Drawing
with charcoal & pastels

Paige Henson

The Rourke Press, Inc.
Vero Beach, Florida 32964

ART CREDITS:
© Eyewire, Inc.: pages 4, 5, 16
Charlie Beyl Kingfish Studios: 8, 10, 11, 12, 13, 14, 15, 16, 17, 18, 19, 21, 22, 26, 27
Jon DiVenti, Kingfish Studios: 20, 23, 24,

PHOTOGRAPHY:
Glen Benson and East Coast Studios

PRODUCED & DESIGNED BY:
East Coast Studios, Merritt Island, Florida

EDITORIAL SERVICES:
Susan Albury

ACKNOWLEDGEMENTS:
East Coast Studios would like to thank Gardendale Elementary School, Merritt Island, for their assistance in this project.

Library of Congress Cataloging-in-Publication Data

Henson, Paige, 1949-
    Drawing with charcoal and pastels / by Paige Henson
        p. cm. — (How to paint and draw)
    Includes bibliographical references and index.
    Summary: Describes the various effects that can be achieved by creating art with charcoal and pastels and provides instructions for selecting and using the appropriate supplies.
    ISBN 1-57103-313-0
    1. Painting—Technique Juvenile literature.   2. Drawing—Technique Juvenile literature. [1. Drawing—Technique. 2. Painting—Technique.] I. Title. II. Series: Henson, Paige, 1949-
How to paint and draw.
ND1500.H47 1999
741.2'2—dc21   99-23527
                                                                      CIP

Printed in the USA

Contents

CHAPTER 1

A French Beginning

In the early 16th century, a French artist developed an amazing new method of dry painting.

The man, Jean Perréal (ZHON PAIR ray all), added a gum base to raw **pigment** (PIG munt), creating sticks of color called soft **pastels** (peh STELZ). Artists of the day like the Italian Leonardo da Vinci (duh VIN chee) (1452-1519) used the new pastel sticks to test how their **chalk** (CHOK) or **charcoal** (CHAHR kohl) sketches might look in color. They could see results immediately, saving all the time and error involved in using slow-drying, "wet" paint.

This is a self-portrait of the Italian artist Leonardo da Vinci.

Later, in the 17th and 18th centuries, pastel pictures became a popular art form. Members of wealthy Parisian families felt it was the "in" thing to have their portraits created by a pastelist. Through the years well-known artists such as Eugene Delacroix (del uh KROY), Edgar Degas (day GAH), Camille Pissarro (puh SAHR o), Berthe Morisot (moh ree ZOH) and American-born Mary Cassatt (kuh SAT) have explored the wonder and magic of pastel painting.

Artist Mary Cassatt (1845-1926) was best known for her many pastels and oils picturing loving mother-and-child pairs. This work is titled "The Bath."

2 Which Pastels to Choose

The word *pastel* is Italian for paste, referring to the paste of chalk, pigment, and gum used to make powdery sticks of color. There are many types of pastels available—soft pastels, hard pastels, **oil pastels** (OYL peh STELZ), chalk pastels, pastel pencils, half (short stick) pastels, large (chunky) pastels, **Conté crayons** (KAHN tay KRAY ahnz) and so forth. Soft pastels give brilliant color and are the most popular with artists because of the easy way they blend and cover the surface of paper. These are the most expensive and fragile of all pastels and should be handled and stored with care. Soft pastels are often sold in boxed sets with foam protectors between each stick so the pastels won't break up and crumble as quickly.

If you work much with pastels, however, you will soon realize that using crumbled bits and broken sticks is part of the creative experience. Hard pastels, Conté crayons, and pastel pencils are not as fragile as soft pastel sticks and are used more as drawing tools than as painting tools. Water-soluble pastels create an interesting effect like watercolor paint when mixed with water. You will probably want to experiment with several different pastel types, as each has its own special qualities and characteristics. Depending on the look you want, you may decide to use one, two, or even three different types of pastels in one picture.

Charcoal is made from animal material or from carbonized wood made by charring willows, vines, or other twigs in airtight containers. You can buy charcoal in long, skinny sticks or in pencil form.

Paper

You can buy paper made especially for pastel drawing and painting, but any paper with texture and some weight to it — such as watercolor, charcoal, or construction paper — will do nicely. Even cardboard is fine. Do not use smooth paper or paper with a slick coating because without ridges it will not "hold" the pastel powder. Colored paper is often used by artists to enhance pastel art, but the most popular choice for pastel work is cream-colored paper. The color you choose depends on the effect you want to create.

Here is how pastel looks drawn on cardboard . . .

and here is how the same picture looks on cream-colored paper.

Here is a list of other tools that can help you create great pastel art:

1 A plywood board on which to mount your paper

2 Easel clips, thumbtacks, or masking tape to hold the paper to the board

3 A kneaded rubber eraser for erasing mistakes and creating special effects

4 A medium-sized paintbrush to remove excess pastel dust from your paper

5 Tissues, wet wipes, or an old cloth keep your fingers clean

6 Cotton balls, cotton swabs, or paper stumps for blending (you may just use your finger)

7 A **fixative** (FIK suh tiv) spray to prevent smearing when you have completed your picture (an adult should assist you)

Color Basics

Primary colors (PRY mehr ee KUH lurz) are red, yellow, and blue. A primary color cannot be made or mixed from any other color. **Secondary colors** (SEH kun dehr ee KUH lurz) are orange, green, and purple and are the result of mixing two primary colors together, like this:

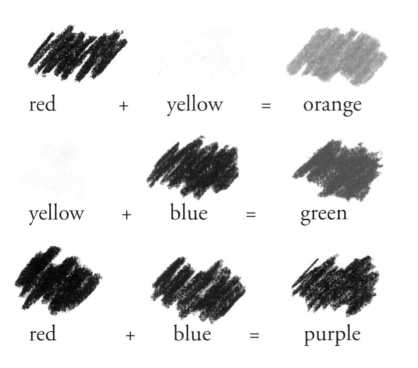

red   +   yellow   =   orange

yellow   +   blue   =   green

red   +   blue   =   purple

Colors are classified as "warm" or "cool." Basically, **warm colors** (WOHRM KUH lurz) are the reds, yellows, and oranges associated with the warmth of the sun; **cool colors** (KOOL KUH lurz) are the blues, purples, and greens of mountains, trees, lakes, and other things associated with nature. In addition to warm and cool colors, there are black, white, and earth **tones** (TOHNZ). A **tint** (TINT) of a color is that color plus white. A tone of a color is that color plus gray. A **shade** (SHAYD) of a color is that color plus black. **Value** (VAL yoo) refers to the lightness or darkness of a color.

Cool Tips

Punch a hole out of the middle of a piece of white bread and knead it with your fingers just a little. Voila! You now have a super eraser that will not "scrub" or scratch your pastel paper.

To remember these warm colors, think of them as colors of the sun and of fire.

To remember cool colors think of the colors that you might use to paint the icy waters of the Arctic regions.

Because you will be applying pastel colors directly to paper instead of mixing them on a palette as you would with paint, you will need a nice range of color and tint choices. Look closely at the sky in this picture. Would you guess that more than seven different pastel colors were used here?

When working with pastels, some smearing will always occur, but you can reduce smearing by turning your paper as you work so that the heel of your hand doesn't rest on the parts you've already drawn.

Terrific Techniques

Mixing and Blending Soft Pastels

You can smudge soft pastels together to **blend** (BLEND) colors, but it is not easy to get the exact color you want by putting one color right on top of the other. An **optical mix** (AHP tah kul MIKS), however, can be made by drawing

lines of one color on top of another so that the color underneath (known as the base color) shows through. The color is then mixed with a viewer's eyes instead of on paper. Here is an example of optical mixing.

If you want to put a light color over a dark color, apply the dark one first and spray it with fixative to "fix" the color. Then apply the lighter color. You may need an adult to help you spray. Remember, never spray anything from an aerosol can if you are in a closed room where no fresh air is circulating!

Always lay the dark color first.

Cool Tips

Put a cup or two of uncooked rice into a small, open box. As you finish with each soft pastel, drop it into the box. The rice will help keep your sticks clean from excess dust and protect them from rolling off the table and breaking.

Blending means spreading the pastel color on the paper after it has been applied. Blending will help your color stay put longer and is a good way to create stains and tones that graduate from dark to light. You can use a cotton ball, a cotton swab, or your fingertips to blend pastels. Just remember that you should rub very gently so you won't remove any of the powdery color or damage the paper.

Edward Degas (day GAH) loved to paint people as they moved about. Because of this he painted many works featuring ballet dancers and other performers in the 19th century. Degas was the first painter to exhibit pastel works as finished art, not just sketches.

Using Harder Pastels

You can draw beautifully with pastel crayons and pencils! Practice first on newspaper to become familiar with how the pencil or crayon works. Use all its points to explore this. Press down softly at first, then a bit harder. Then harder still. Use your kneaded eraser to lighten up some of the darker shades you create. Remember that pastel pencils are harder than sticks, making them ideal for adding detail to your pastel art. You can also use a drawing technique called **cross-hatching** (KRAHS hach ing) that involves making small lines cross over one another to color in an area and give it texture.

Making Marks

It is a good idea to become familiar with the marks made by the pastels you have chosen. With soft pastels, practice using all the edges of the sticks, then make broader strokes by using the  whole length of the stick. Notice that if you press too hard, the stick will crumble. Square pastels will make different marks than rounded ones, pencils will make more detailed marks than sticks, and so on. Try to keep the heel of your hand raised off the paper to prevent too much smearing.

Pastel Stencils

STEP 1
Use a cutout shape of something you like—an animal, a heart, or something similar. Put the shape down on paper and rub the edges heavily with a soft pastel stick.

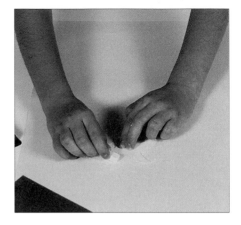

STEP 2
Carefully place the shape on a piece of construction paper, hold it firmly, and with a tissue wrapped around your index finger, brush the loose color powder away from the shape and onto the paper.

STEP 3
Remove the shape and you have created an interesting pastel stencil. Have an adult help you spray your design with fixative.

Oil Pastels

Oil pastels come in small, soft sticks, somewhat like crayons. They will give your artwork the moist look of an oil painting if you use them thickly and "build up" the color on your paper. Because of their unique texture, oil pastels are great for blending and shading, too. Be careful, however, not to go overboard or your blended colors may end up looking like a muddy mixture. If you make a mistake, just scrape as much off as possible with your fingernail and erase the rest with a kneaded eraser. Oil pastels get softer and more fluid as they warm in your hand, so it's better to use them in their original wrappers for as long as you can. Oil pastels

may take a little more practice to master than basic pastels, but you will enjoy the results. Because of the texture of these special pastels, avoid spraying your finished art with fixative.

CHAPTER 5

Charcoal and Chalk

Charcoal is a great drawing and outlining tool to use with some of your pastel pictures because it can create the same smearing and blending effect of soft pastels. Charcoal lead is very soft and creates a rich velvety line of black color that can easily be blended. Like soft pastels, the sticks are extremely breakable and can create quite a mess if not handled properly, so keep a cleanup cloth handy. Be sure to keep loose charcoal powder away from the parts of your picture you wish to remain white.

20

White charcoal is a chalklike pencil that is soft enough to cover large areas of colored paper. It can also be applied over charcoal for a brilliant special effect.

Try Drawing a Zebra

STEP 1 Using white charcoal, lightly sketch the outline of a zebra on construction paper.

STEP 2 Next, draw in the white areas to create the ears, mane, tail, and stripes.

STEP 3 Draw in the black areas last using black charcoal—the hooves, nose area, details in the mane and tail, the eye, and black stripes.

Light and Shade

To figure out where highlights and shadows should be added to your drawing, think of a beam of light or sunshine shining down from the top left side of your picture.

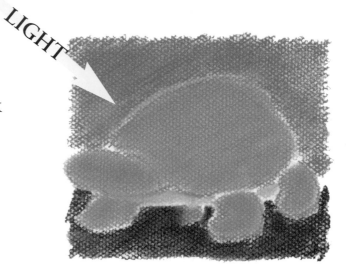

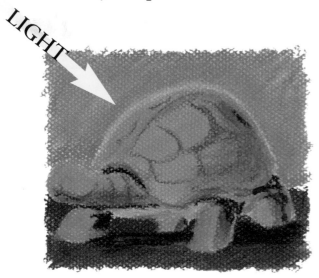

Where would the shadows fall?

Where would the light shine on the object, making it brighter?

22

Once you have added all the details, look again at what more could be shaded or highlighted to add depth. One way to highlight areas in your picture is to use your kneaded eraser to remove some of the pigment.

PROJECT

Using the side of your charcoal stick, cover an entire page heavily with charcoal. Now, with the tip of your kneaded eraser or a chunk of white bread formed to a point, make lines to create a "picture in reverse" by removing some of the charcoal pigment. This is a very messy project, so be sure to take time to clean up well!

White chalk on black construction paper can create quite a dramatic look. Think of other objects that would look "cool" drawn this way. A haunted house. A mysterious black cat?

CHAPTER 7

Sidewalk Art

Sidewalk chalk comes in boxes or big plastic buckets and can open up worlds of outdoor fun. You can draw colorful gameboards, sports boundaries, artwork, or hopscotch courts by the dozens, and all of it will be washed away with the first good rain. Even though the chalk marks don't last forever, it's still a good idea to ask permission before drawing outdoors.

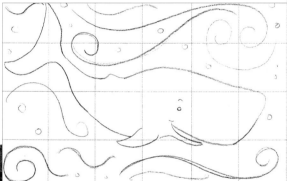

Drawing your art with a grid on paper first can be a helpful guide when creating sidewalk art. Use the grid drawn on your paper to help you match what goes in which square of your grid on the sidewalk art.

Try Drawing a Dinosaur

STEP 1

Sketch in an outline of your dinosaur. (Remember to use a grid if you think it will help.)

STEP 2

Lay down the large areas of the base colors you want to use.

STEP 3

Blend your base colors with lighter and darker colors to create shadows, highlights, or an interesting sky or background.

Try Drawing an Enchanted Castle

STEP 1

Sketch in an outline of your castle.

STEP 2

Lay down large areas of the base colors you want to use.

STEP 3

Blend your base colors with lighter and darker colors to create shadows and highlights. You can use a dark pastel to add more detail as a finishing touch.

Cleanup

Once you have scooped up your pastel crumbles, cleaned off your hands, and applied fixative to your picture with adult help, you are ready to preserve your art creation. Remember, never roll up a pastel work—use an overlay instead.

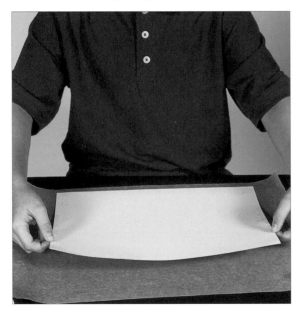

STEP 1 Tear off a piece of waxed paper and lay it on a table. Place your art face down on the waxed paper.

STEP 2 Fold the top edge of the waxed paper over the top of your art and hold it there with two pieces of masking tape. This overlay will help protect your pastel picture.

Be sure to place your pastel sticks, crayons, or pens carefully in their original containers so they will be ready for your next art project.

Save your charcoal and pastel crumbles and keep them in small containers. You can dab this dust with a cotton ball or your fingertip and apply it to your pictures where you want to create a textured, grainy look.

Have your friends lie on the patio or sidewalk (make sure no passersby are coming!) and trace around their bodies with chalk. Tell them to strike poses as if they were being very active: diving into a pool, jumping over a bridge, making a long football pass, etc. Be sure they lie very still as you trace them in "motion."

Glossary

blend (BLEND) — to mix colors together by rubbing one pastel onto another

chalk (CHOK) — a soft limestone composed of minute seashells

charcoal (CHAHR kohl) — carbonized wood made by charring willow, vine, or other twigs

conté crayons (KAHN tay KRAY ahnz) — chalk-based pastels; a cross between soft & hard pastels

cool colors (KOOL KUH lurz) — "icy" colors such as greens, blues, purples

cross-hatching (KRAHS hach ing) — crossing small, closely-spaced lines over one another to create texture and tone

fixative (FIK suh tiv) — chemical substance that allows pastels, charcoals, or other soft particles to become "fixed" to paper; fixative prevents smearing

oil pastels (OYL peh STELZ) —pastels whose pigments are bound by oil, not by gum

optical mix (AHP tah kul MIKS)— lines or dots of different colors placed so closely together that the viewer sees them as merged into another, singular color

pastel (peh STEL) — Italian word meaning "paste"; sticks or pencils with their pigment bound together by oil or a gum compound; comes in several forms including soft and hard pastels

pigment (PIG munt) — substance that gives paints or pastels their color

primary colors (PRY mehr ee KUH lurz)— red, yellow and blue; primary colors cannot be mixed from other colors

secondary colors (SEH kun dehr ee KUH lurz) — two primary colors mixed together to create orange, green or purple

shade (SHAYD) — one color plus black

tint (TINT) — one color plus white

tone (TOHN) — one color plus gray

value (VAL yoo) — the lightness or darkness of a color

warm colors (WOHRM KUH lurz)— "sunny" colors such as reds, oranges, yellows

Index

Further Reading

- Brookes, Mona, *Drawing with Children*, G.P. Putnam's Sons, 1996.
- Cummings, Pat, *Talking with Artists*, Simon & Schuster, 1992.
- Cummings, Pat, *Talking with Artists* Vol. II, Simon & Schuster, 1995.
- Kohl, Maryann, *Preschool Art*, Gryphon House,1994.
- Martin, Judy, editorial consultant, *Painting and Drawing*, Millbrook Press,1993.
- Mason, Antony, *Picasso*, Barron's Educational Publishers,1994.
- Thompson, Kimberly Boehler and Loftus, Diana Standing, *Art Connections*, GoodYearBooks, 1995.
- Wright, Michael, *An Introduction to Pastels*, Dorling Kindersley Publishers, 1993.
- *Learning to Paint in Pastels,* Barron's Educational Publishers, 1997.